How to Analyze People

- The Ultimate Guide to Speed Reading People Through Proven Psychological Techniques, Body Language Analysis and Personality Types and Patterns •

By Sebastian Croft

Copyright © 2018

Table of Contents

The Endless Mystery of the Human Mind 4

Why Analyze a Person? 7

Becoming an Analyst of People 11

Figuring Out the Basics: Understanding Personality Types 14

Analyzing Personality Types 16

    Introversion Versus Extraversion 17

    Sensing Versus Intuition 20

    Thinking Versus Feeling 22

    Judging Versus Perceiving 23

Putting the Personality Puzzle Together 26

    INTJ – The Architect 27

    ENTP – The Visionary 28

    INTP – The Philosopher 30

    ENTJ – The Leader 31

    INFJ – The Protector 33

    ENFP – The Organizer 35

    INFP – The Mediator 36

    ENFJ – The Protagonist 37

    ISFJ – The Defender 38

    ESFJ – The Provider 40

    ISTJ – The Facilitator 41

    ESTJ – The Executive 43

    ISFP – The Artist 44

    ESFP – The Entertainer 45

    ISTP – The Engineer 46

    ESTP – The Entrepreneur 48

The Things that Make Us Unique 50

Firstborn, Second Born, Baby of the Family: The Role of Birth Order 55

    First Child 55

    Middle Child 56

    Last Child 56

    Only Child 56

A Person's Beliefs 58

Cold Readings 61

Reading Body Language 65

Detecting Specific Personality Traits Through Body Language 74

Detecting Lies 81

Danger Signals 84

A Final Word: Listening to Really Hear 89

The Endless Mystery of the Human Mind

Human beings are fascinating creatures, complicated to the point of lunacy yet achingly simple at the same time. No two human beings think alike, nor have the same experience of life to base their opinions on, nor make the same decisions in the spur of the moment, yet we are all driven by the same desires: love, safety, comfort and so on. We take different paths to the same conclusion, each of us as unique as a star in the sky.

So how, as an onlooker, can you possibly analyze even one human being? Should it not take days, weeks, months to understand what makes that person tick and predict how they are likely to react?

Not necessarily. To understand human beings, you must first acknowledge that all of us are just points on a range of bell curves. Each of those bell curves represents a characteristic or trait – optimism, empathy, kindness and so on.

You may be as kind as it's possible to be, you may be as cruel as it's possible to be or (more likely) you fall somewhere in between. You could be more quick to anger than anyone else, you might be the slowest to anger of anyone, or (more likely) you fall somewhere in between.

If you're not familiar with the bell curve, it's called that because it's a hump with the largest portion in the middle. At either end are the outliers – the smallest number of people will meet those standards. Most of us lie somewhere near the center of the bell curve, at the highest point, or skewed slightly to its left or right.

When you begin to understand that we are all simply a collection of characteristics, each of them interacting with one another to produce a unique personality, it suddenly becomes easier to accept that reading and analyzing a human being is possible.

So how do you do it, and why would you want to? We'll take a closer look at these questions as we begin to dive into this crucial skill.

Within these pages, you are going to learn how to tell when a person is reacting well to your words or when you have bored, angered or annoyed them. You'll be able to spot signs of discomfort and know how to reassure or relax.

You'll be able to convince people of your arguments more efficiently and win them over to your side.

You'll know how to read a person's body language and understand what they aren't saying just as fully as what they are saying.

All these things and more will be revealed to you as you explore the human psyche. It's one of the most interesting journeys you are ever likely to take...

Why Analyze a Person?

If you're reading this book, it's because the title caught your attention and reading other people is something you are interested to be able to do. But have you asked yourself why? Do you know what benefits this skill can bring?

Most of us think we're pretty good at telling what other people are thinking. Indeed, some of us do have that skill naturally – and, for others, it's culturally ingrained. Cultures that frown on speaking one's mind tend to be better at reading signals than those where airing feelings is perfectly acceptable, for example.

But having a talent and knowing how to use it are two different things. You might have perfect pitch, but it still takes practice to sing like an angel; you may have an instinctive understanding of mechanics, but you still can't fix a car until you've memorized each of its parts.

Analyzing other people is something that takes work and attention, but you'll be surprised at just how many benefits you'll reap. Such as:

- Clarity – No more confusion when dealing with people who think very differently to you – and no more confusion when they don't react as you would and you attempts to befriend, convince or explain fall flat on their face.

- Effectiveness – When you are able to read another person's signals, you are also able to adjust your words and behavior accordingly. This, in turn, allows you to convey your message more clearly and effectively, which will more often lead to the outcome you were hoping for.

- Relationships – Some of us are more naturally awkward than others and find it tough to make new friends and impress acquaintances. When you can read other people, you can tell how they feel about you, understand what makes them happy and what they enjoy and communicate with them more deeply.

- Safety – Not every interaction is positive. Sometimes, you will find yourself dealing with hostile human beings who either mean you harm or are angered and likely to lash out. Knowing how to look for these signs and size up a potentially dangerous person in a single instant can mean the difference between safety and danger.

- Success – You won't just know how to read your peers, you will also be able to glean what your superiors are thinking. You'll know what impresses your boss and what annoys him or her, you'll know how to build relationships within your workplace and you'll feel more confident when presenting your ideas.

- Confidence – If you are an introvert or shy, you probably dread the idea of large social gatherings and avoid networking opportunities like the plague. When you can read people, these occasions become much less daunting – indeed, you might actually find yourself enjoying those random conversations with strangers!

- Altruism – Reading other people is not all about what you can do for yourself. It's also about what you can do for other people. You will learn how to set people at their ease, tell when they are in need of something that they can't or won't tell you about and, perhaps most importantly, how to understand them and their needs, hopes and desires. There is no greater gift you can offer to another human being than understanding and acceptance of who they are and willingness to provide what they are looking for.

Becoming an Analyst of People

If it's as easy as I'm suggesting to read other people, how come not everybody is doing it? Surely we would all be checking off mental lists at the beginning of every interaction and proving ourselves effective communicators every single time?

Obviously, that's not the case, or there would never be a single misunderstanding. A good analyst must possess certain traits in order for their skills to work in the field.

So, before we begin to develop those skills, let's first concentrate on who you, the analyst, must become. Some of these traits will come to you more naturally than others because, just like every other human being, you are unique. To be effective, however, you will need to hone these skills to a fine point:

- First, you must be good at paying attention to details. You need to spot the little things just as quickly as you do the big ones. If you think this skill needs work, try taking a walk down a familiar road near your home. Let your eyes wander across every surface in every direction, drilling down to the littlest of details as well as drinking in the view as a whole. How many things did you notice that you have never spotted before? How many times were you surprised by an entire building you've never noticed, signs of decay you hadn't picked up or little features that hadn't caught your attention? The more you try this exercise, in both unfamiliar places and locations you thought you knew like the back of your hand, the more you will hone your attention to detail.

- Second, you must become an observer. That means knowing you are not here to change what you are looking at, you are only here to catalog and understand it. The only thing in this picture that you can or should try to change is your own role within it. Before you can do that, you must observe fully and deeply and gather all the information you can.

- Third, you must set aside any instinct to judge. Placing a value on cruelty versus kindness, laziness versus drive or passivity versus forcefulness will not help you here. Accept that people are who they are and that it is not your place to try to change that. Let go of your emotional reaction to these traits – you must be objective to be a good analyst.

- Finally, learn to listen. Some of us are better at this than others. Begin your practice now: the next time you hold a conversation with someone, avoid every temptation to speak. Just listen. Obviously, it wouldn't be a conversation if you stayed completely silent, but try to keep the emphasis on what that person wants to tell you and your own contributions all about encouraging them to keep talking. Ask questions, ask for clarifications, simply make noises and gestures of acknowledgement. Maintain eye contact and really listen to what they are saying. The more you do this, the more you will learn from them – and the more they will appreciate being listened to.

Figuring Out the Basics: Understanding Personality Types

Psychologists have spent decades trying to boil humanity down into categories. The result has been to create broad classes of people to capture all that diversity we boast as a species.

The personality types are important to an analyst, but it's also crucial to remember that no person is going to fit into a category perfectly. Just because person A is an introvert doesn't make them exactly the same as person B. Other factors will come into play, altering how that person thinks and feels sometimes dramatically.

Person A, for example, may also be highly intuitive, while person B is not. When you interact with person A, it's hard to tell that they don't feel all that comfortable with social occasions because their intuition is helping them understand how to converse with you. Person B, on the other hand, does not have that benefit and seems awkward and uncomfortable.

That single example illustrates how the convergence of different personality traits leads to an individual, utterly unique human being – but it's only one example of thousands. A kind person who is outgoing will more likely stop in the street to help you; a kind but shy person might be more likely to send you an anonymous gift through the mail. A person who is a born leader and patient will be an entirely different kind of boss in the workplace than one who is impatient.

The list goes on and on, but the point is made: as an analyst, you're looking for as full a picture as you can gather of the person you are hoping to read, and you may not have very long to put that picture together.

That's why it's so important to understand the personality types. They can give you a basis to work with – a starting point. It can be more than enough in a fleeting, chance encounter, especially if you have learned how to overlay observations of such things as body language and context.

For those people you already know well or would like to know better, you have much more time to build a full picture. Over the top of that personality matrix, you will be able to layer your ongoing knowledge of cultural differences, social differences and the experience that has shaped that person into who they are.

Analyzing Personality Types

We'll begin our journey by learning the personality types – the basic structure of your analysis. Think of this as the scaffolding; how close to completing the building you get will depend on how much time and effort you put into fleshing out the picture.

Of all the many personality systems that have been suggested over the years, the one that has proved most reliable and accurate is the Myers Briggs. This particular system looks at four bell curves and places a person somewhere on the scale for each. This, in turn, provides 16 potential combinations that lead to a personality description.

The four traits in question are:

- Introversion versus extraversion
- Intuition versus sensing
- Thinking versus feeling
- Judging versus perceiving.

Though the traditional Myers Briggs test involves a questionnaire, it's entirely possible to calculate where a person falls on each of these bell curves without asking them a single question.

To do so, you simply need to calculate where they fall on the scale of each of these four dichotomies. A person cannot be both introverted and extraverted; nor can they be thinking and feeling at the same time.

Let's take a look at each of the four in turn:

Introversion Versus Extraversion

An introvert only has so much energy to give at one time to social interactions, while an extravert actually derives their energy from such occasions. In other words, an extravert thrives on interaction and is likely to be talkative, gregarious and comfortable in large social situations, taking pleasure in any activity that involves other people.

An introvert, on the other hand, is more reserved and reflected and derives their energy from reflection. This energy is then spent during social interactions and eventually dwindles, requiring time alone for more reflection to replenish.

It's not that one of these two classes likes people and the other doesn't: the difference is in the source of energy. Think of it as spending as opposed to earning; at a party, an extravert is earning their energy, while an introvert is spending it. When in their own company, an introvert is earning and an extravert is spending.

This can manifest in very different ways, as you might expect. An introvert is likely to have hobbies such as reading, gaming and spending time in nature, where an extravert would balk at the idea of so much alone time and prefers community events, gatherings and parties.

It's easy to mistake shyness for introversion and vice versa and it's not uncommon for introverts to get a bad rap as "anti-social" – understandable for a species that is hypersocial and finds it difficult to fully understand someone who prefers their own company.

Both ends of this spectrum have their positive and negative sides. For an extravert, popularity and being the "life of the party" tends to be rewarding for those around them as well as themselves and they are often found at the heart of a community.

To find an extravert, look for the person whose idea it was to host a chili cook-off and who is making the rounds of the guests making small talk and laughing. Look for the person who was first to arrive and has an almost magnetic attraction for others, or the one who most readily signs up for business initiatives and political groups. An extravert thrives in such conditions and is easy to spot right at the center of the action.

An introvert feels considerably less comfortable in these situations but, on the other hand, thrives in the kinds of activity that require contemplation and deep thought. Writers, artists, scientists – even leaders, in situations where the goal is to change the world rather than personal gain.

This can be the easiest of the four dichotomies to spot. Take a look at the person's body language: if it is open and relaxed with signs of happiness and contentment while at the center of a crowd or group of people, and their voice is raised with little regard for who might overhear, you are likely dealing with an extravert. The more people attracted to that person's innate charisma, the more extraverted they are likely to be.

A person who prefers to be near the edges of the crowd and is showing the body language signals of prey rather than predator (closed arms, lack of eye contact, stiff limbs, positioned to avoid as much attention as possible, quiet speaking voice) is your introvert. The more uncomfortable they seem, the more introverted.

Sensing Versus Intuition

The second dichotomy is a little more complicated to understand, but equally important to a person's overall character. Intuition is the ability to know about something even in the absence of tangible proof, which can allow a person to sense what's coming down the road. An intuitive person relies on their gut feeling and looks more at the big picture than the details, preferring to consider the possibility of the future than the reality of the present moment.

Such a person tends to be innovative and likes to buck the trend, finding creative solutions to problems and analyzing situations quickly and productively. Logic is not the main driving force; rather, they rely on gut instinct to drive their decisions.

Sensory people, on the other hand, are only interested in what their senses are telling them. Their decisions are driven by what they can see, hear, feel, touch and taste and a conscious analysis of these things. Data is more important than subconscious feelings and decisions are rarely made in the absence of proof. Logic is the driving force, as is practicality, and a sensory person is more likely to stick to tried and tested methods than suggest new ones.

How can you tell if the person you are speaking to is intuitive or sensory? The two personality types will enjoy very different types of conversation.

Test this out by asking the person how their day has gone and listen hard to the types of observations they make. A sensory person will focus on the things they sensed – what they heard people say, what they saw and what color it was, how loud the music was in the elevator. An intuitive person will not give so many details and will likely give a shorter answer, as the minutiae of the day was not what they were focusing on.

Now, ask that same person an abstract question – something about their views on politics, social justice, religion, anything that is more about considering an issue than observing what is around them. An intuitive will jump on this and begin a conversation that could easily last for hours, exploring new ideas and tapping you for your own opinions, but a sensory will grow tired of it after not too long at all.

In essence, a sensory is able to discuss pop culture, the latest social gathering, their day at work or anything else where their strong powers of perception come into play for hours on end, while an intuitive can explore the unknown and intangible much more readily, finding "big ideas" more meaningful and rewarding.

Thinking Versus Feeling

This dichotomy concerns how a person makes their decisions. A thinker does so based on facts and principles, looking at the logic of a situation and weighing up the positive and negatives sides and searching for explanations. In other words, the driving force behind their decisions is their brain and the emotional impact is given second fiddle.

Thinkers are direct and straightforward, focused on fairness and telling the truth, no matter how that affects the person they are talking to. The human element of a scenario is not as important to a thinker as the logical facts in front of them.

A feeling person is more driven by their emotions and how a decision will make them feel, rather than the stark logic of the situation. The driving force behind their decisions is their heart.

This does not just apply to their own emotions, either: a feeling person will bear in mind the emotional impact that their decision could have on those around them, too. They are compassionate and tactful, preferring to save someone's feelings rather than give them the cold, hard truth. These are the idealists of the world, who prefer to create harmony and happiness wherever they go.

When speaking to a thinker, you'll notice that they are interested in facts and figures. If you are selling to a thinker, for instance, you'll find they want to know about the price, the different options available and similarity to another recent purchase. A feeler, on the other hand, wants to know more about how their purchase will look and feel, how it will fit into their lives and the lives of their loved ones and what kind of person likes the different options.

In a more general conversation, a thinker is likely to gather facts from you – what you do, where you live, who you are related to. They are brief and concise and their words are straightforward. A feeler, on the other hand, will want to know more about how you feel and what you are thinking as they attempt to empathize with you more strongly. They will come across as friendlier and warmer and will be more open about themselves – expecting the same from you in return.

Judging Versus Perceiving
The final dichotomy concerns how a person interacts with the world around them and how they deal with the stress and strain of life.

A judging person is organized and capable of planning ahead, preparing for outcomes ahead of time and great at meeting deadlines. They focus well and stick between the lines of the careful plans they make.

Those who fall into the judging category often make lists of things to do and prefer to get their work finished before turning their attention to recreation. They rarely procrastinate until the last minute, portioning out their workloads evenly. On the other hand, they can tend to focus so much on a goal that they ignore new information along the way to it.

A perceiving person, on the other hand, is entirely more flexible and can adapt to changes along the way much more easily. They are more comfortable making decisions without any specific facts and plans available and enjoy experimenting.

Those who fall into this category stay open to new information and prefer not to make plans wherever possible. They swap between work and play, completing their work in bursts of energy rather than allocated blocks. On the other hand, they can sometimes stay so open to new information that they miss making decisions when decisions are needed.

The difference is mainly about structure. While a judging person likes structure and concrete plans, a perceiving person prefers to be spontaneous and adapt along the way.

When speaking with a judging person, you'll notice that they have everything figured out for their future plans. If you suggest an activity, their first impulse will be to ask when, where and how long it will last. A perceiving person, on the other hand, will ask if you feel like leaving right now and will be easy and open to a different suggestion.

Judging people often come across as more rigid, while perceiving people seem eager to just go with the flow. A judging person might actually appear uncomfortable at a proposal that doesn't come with detailed information, though whether a person is judging or perceiving doesn't actually affect their eagerness to indulge in an activity. On the contrary: suggest a day of ice skating to either type and they're equally likely to love the idea. The judging person is just going to want to know precisely what your plans are to make it happen.

Putting the Personality Puzzle Together

It's worth stressing again at this point that figuring out the four personality corners of a person is not going to tell you precisely who they are and what they are thinking. Their culture, background, experience and other factors are all going to play into the equation, making two people who theoretically fall into the category follow very different life paths.

Think of the 16 personality types as fences around a field. By identifying which one you are dealing with, you know they are somewhere within that field, but never precisely where. Some intrepid souls might even have one leg outside the fence in another field altogether.

But the fence does give you a boundary to work within, and that's where it comes in so handy for an analyst. You can begin with the personality type you have identified and use it to dig for even more information about how that person's individual character has evolved since they were born.

So, taking the four different personality dichotomies we identified in the previous chapter, the person you are analyzing will fall into one of 16 categories. Each is defined by four letters representing which side they fell on each of the dichotomies:

- E – Extraversion
- I – Introversion
- S – Sensing
- N – Intuition
- T – Thinking
- F – Feeling
- J – Judgement
- P – Perception

INTJ – The Architect

The INTJ is truly independent and thoroughly analytical. They prefer to work alone and are one of the least sociable of all the personality types. On the other hand, if nobody else seems capable of leading, they will do so. They are both logical and creative but have a low tolerance for propaganda and spin and are not accepting of authority unless it has been earned.

Architects prefer a structured lifestyle with timetables and clearly defined decisions. Their curiosity is perhaps their defining characteristic – they are fascinated with how things work and constantly seeking knowledge and information.

An architect is not great at small talk and polite conversation, preferring to talk about things that "matter". They can sometimes seem smug, as they know a lot of things about a lot of things and are never afraid to share them. They will not seem overly emotional, however, and are not keen on following social norms in the form of rituals designed to put those around them at ease.

At their happiest when given the freedom to work independently and find their own solutions, they are known for coming up with creative answers and are often found within an academic, consulting or management role. On first meeting an Architect, you will likely find them intimidating and perhaps somewhat cold, though rest assured that this personality type is a loyal friend or partner to those their intuition tells them are worth their time.

ENTP – The Visionary

This personality type can see the connections between all things, whether that's people, ideas or things. This also enables them to see how those connections can be improved.

Outgoing and enthusiastic, the Visionary's motives come from a desire to understand and then improve the world around them. They enjoy a good debate, loving the chance to look at an idea from every angle while applying just as much of that enthusiasm to each side of an argument.

One thing you may quickly notice about the Visionary is that they are unlikely to spare your feelings on their path to understanding. To the Visionary, it's more important to truly understand than it is to spare your feelings. Visionaries can get under your skin and will ask you the difficult questions, even if they sense you are uncomfortable.

The Visionary has big ideas thanks to this way of thinking, but is less adept at actually carrying them through, as he or she will have very little interest in the finer details. Expect a person in this category to dream very big dreams and want to debate them at every opportunity.

While a Visionary is never going to be the most popular person in the room thanks to that disregard for social niceties, but listening to them carefully can be thoroughly rewarding.

There is no problem too big, no matter too small that they will not throw that immense imagination into unraveling – with plenty of fascinating conversation along the way, if you can steel yourself against their indomitable pursuit of the truth.

INTP – The Philosopher

At the other end of the scale from the Visionary is the Philosopher, whose introverted nature leads them to apply that same deep curiosity in a more isolated manner. They, too, want to know how things work and are interested in finding creative solutions, which means you'll most likely discover they have followed a career path in the sciences, architecture, law or philosophy.

Not too keen on blindly following authority, the Philosopher is also the most keenly logical of all the personalities. This personality type is intellectual and innovative, irritated by inconsistencies and able to see things from multiple perspectives.

A Philosopher often seems distracted, as much of the work being done by their minds is silent and kept internal. They do not need to talk through their solutions and how they got there, though they will happily do so with an engaged audience or peer.

In a social situation, the Philosopher will be happy in a circle of people they respect and charming to spend time with. The same is not true for large gatherings of unfamiliar faces, however, where you will most likely find this person in the darkest and most isolated corner. They won't balk at the chance for interaction, but it won't be small talk that puts them at their ease – they would much prefer a grand discussion of one of life's great mysteries.

The danger of engaging in such a discussion if you are unfamiliar with the topic, however, is that the Philosopher has very little time for viewpoints that have not been thoroughly thought through and are not patient with those of a lesser intellect than their own. This personality type may not be good at understanding emotions and applying them to a situation, but a Philosopher is great at seeking a logical answer to your problems.

ENTJ – The Leader

It's always easy to spot the Alpha in the room, and nine times out of ten you'll find that they fit into this very distinctive category. This person leads and the rest of the world is expected to follow – they can't help it, it's written in their very DNA.

Focused firmly on goals, the Leader is great at finding the best and most efficient way to get there. They can be visionary, but also realistic in putting together plans. They are independent souls who are hard to influence when making decisions and extremely logical, which can make it difficult for them to build emotion and subjective reality into their thinking.

Unsurprisingly, you'll find the Leader in a business environment most commonly, although they may appear anywhere that a strong leader is required and are often found in politics. They can be extremely intimidating but also magnetically charming, as their confidence is inspirational to others.

A Leader likes a good challenge and is equipped to meet it in a full frontal attack. Their strong will and ability to maintain focus makes them perfect choices to push a group of people towards a common goal while making those people genuinely believe it can be done.

Leaders prefer the company of their peers, loving the experience of sharpening their own weapons on the lodestone of others who think the same way. However, as natural team builders, they are also very quick to spot the positive qualities in others and know exactly how to put them to good use.

Don't expect to be given much quarter for your own shortcomings or emotional reactions from a Leader – they are not fans of weakness and not superb at understanding the feelings of others. If you are lazy at heart, you won't win the affections of the Leader – but if you are determined to be the best that you can in whatever field or role you choose, they will respect and support you without question.

INFJ – The Protector

An extremely rare personality type – only one person in 100 will fall into this category – the Protector is also the most complex and perhaps the most sensitive. This is the personality type most apt to ask, "What is the meaning of life?"

But while they are indeed dreamers, Protectors are also doers. They combine these two seemingly contradictory personality elements into an ability to both see a problem in the world and do something about it.

The Protector won't be the person pushing a daisy into the gun of a soldier – they will be the person on the podium, inspiring others to understand the issue at hand and make change in the world. As you might imagine, you'll often find this personality type in a Martin Luther King Jr. or Gandhi leadership role, aiming to make the world a better place.

As they are adept at fitting in socially, many people mistake the Protector for an extrovert, but actually this skill comes from a genuine interest in people and an intense drive to address the well being of others.

The Protector is a true introvert who needs time away from other people to recharge – but often forgets this.

Protectors are the instruments of change, boasting an impeccable moral compass and an impressive ability to inspire others to follow it. Like the Leader, the Protector has a magnetic quality that attracts others to their side to help them push for the change they so strongly believe must be achieved.

A Protector's conviction in their own beliefs contrasts with their urge to put others before themselves. However, because at heart the Protector believes unshakably in humanity and holds qualities such as compassion and justice on a pedestal, they approach problems from an idealistic perspective that can sway even the hardest of hearts to their cause.

Deep, mysterious and extremely complex, a Protector will seek a role that will help them improve the human condition. They are organized, orderly and independent and enjoy a harmonious team environment. You may find that this person is a healthcare professional or counselor or, on the other hand, has followed a creative career that allows them to express themselves and their creativity. Elegant writers and organized thinkers, Protectors can flourish in any of these fields but will do best when they can contribute to humanity's well-being on a personal level.

ENFP – The Organizer

This personality type can connect with other people like no other and is compelled to seek social activity as often as possible. You'll find yourself attracted to an Organizer as a friend or partner very easily – and you'll find it easy to form a bond with them.

The smile on an Organizer's face is contagious, as is their energy and drive. These are initiators of change – the people who make those around them keen and willing to pursue a goal simply because of the joy and excitement that doing so embodies.

Like the Protector, the Organizer can see behind the curtain of what others are saying. They are incredibly perceptive and adept at reading body language and other signals, which skill they most often use to create harmony and happiness and bind people in a common cause.

While their charm and magnetism does make organizers fantastic leaders, they often fall down when it comes to the monotonous movements towards a goal. They prefer finding creative solutions and challenging the status quo, innovating wherever they can.

An Organizer loves a good party, but has just as much love for a quiet evening with one or two close friends, getting to know them on a deeper level. Their ability to understand others on a sensitive and emotional level gives them an unparalleled ability to win friends and influence people – everyone loves to hang out with an Organizer.

INFP – The Mediator

Another rare personality type, the Mediator is the real idealist of this world, always looking for the best in people and events even when the rest of us cannot see it. This personality is guided by principles more than logic and has a deep need to follow a path of honor and virtue.

You'll have a hard time convincing a Mediator that the world around them is a wonderful place and everyone in it has the capacity for goodness. Though introverts who do not seek social interactions as much as other personality types – and who can feel incredibly uncomfortable in crowds of unfamiliar faces – Mediators are heartwarming companions who can maintain a moral heart within a group of people.

Loyalty and idealism are the Mediator's most obvious characteristics and you will most often find them in roles that allow them to pursue their deeply held beliefs. They make wonderful diplomats and peacemakers and have a gift for communication that helps them mediate through a strong understanding of others.

Unlike the Protector, you won't find this personality type driving the engine of change – but you will find them loyally following the charge. Spending time with a Mediator can remind you of all the beauty in this world and the possibilities ahead of humanity should we choose the path of virtue and harmony. Often artists or engaged in altruistic careers, such as working for charities, these are the people who inspire a warm glow in others' hearts and make us look to the future with optimism.

ENFJ – The Protagonist

Another born leader, the Protagonist oozes passion for their cause and the charisma that attracts others to their side. This is the category that politicians most often fall into, but also teachers and coaches and other professions that require leadership through the sharing of a vision.

A Protagonist is interested in other people almost to a level that can damage them, as it often leads them to get too involved in other people's problems and crises or place trust where it does not belong.

It's that caring for other people, however, that makes the Protagonist the most popular of all the leadership categories. It's another very rare category that only comprises two in every hundred people, which is precisely why this personality type is so often recognized publically for their work.

This is the personality type that will win awards of excellence in teaching or will sweep elections. Their secret lies in their genuine passion and honest interest in others' well being. Empathy is their strong suit, but it can also be their downfall if directed towards a dishonest target looking to take advantage of their good nature.

When the Protagonist speaks, the world sits down to listen. As a politician, the Protagonist wins huge popularity through their deep belief that a solution should always benefit as many people as is possible and should always seek to make the world a better place.

ISFJ – The Defender
A Defender is a walking contradiction, and it's in this that they will most often find their strength. Though they are sensitive souls, they possess the ability to be analytical. Though they are socially reserved, they are well liked by others thanks to their people skills.

Though they are conservative, they do not fear change. The Defender is a large category, with almost 13 percent of the population falling within it, and many of those who boast this personality can be found in the kind of career that has a sense of tradition, such as teaching, charity work and medicine.

Perfectionists and procrastinators, you can nevertheless rely on a Defender to get the job done. A Defender wants to be helpful and useful and embodies the trait of kindness, which makes this personality type a pillar of support for the community as a whole. He or she will go above and beyond to make sure the job has been done and that everyone is happy and accounted for.

Team players and extremely supportive as friends, lovers and colleagues, the Defender wants you to be happy – and will do whatever it takes to make that happen. They do like to be recognized for what they have done, but they will not actively seek that recognition. This personality type will be the first to offer to get something done, but is often forgotten when it comes time to hand out the accolades.

Defenders are often taken advantage of as they believe in the goodness of people and cannot help themselves when it comes to being supportive and giving. A Defender will remember your sister's name and where you last went on vacation and will give you gifts that are incredibly thoughtful. As you can imagine, this makes them valuable friends – but easily hurt when their friendship is taken advantage of. On the other hand, they are liked by almost everybody and this allows them to lead a rewarding life, as it gives them plenty of opportunity to be kind, giving and helpful.

ESFJ – The Provider
This personality type makes everyone around them smile, and they do it by being a cheerleader. Only slightly smaller as a group than the Defenders, they are happy and cheerful and enjoy making the world a fun place to live.

You'll notice that the Provider is very interested in bringing everyone together, whether it's for a party of a reunion or a holiday. What they want most of all is to see the people they care about look happy.

They don't mesh well with the personality types who favor introspective and philosophical debate – they are much more interested in gossip and pop culture for the simple reason that these things allow them to know what is going on around them and how best to contribute in a way that will bring a smile.

This isn't a category known for creative thought and innovation, but a Provider will respect the authority around them and live within the rules that have been imposed. Making waves, after all, does not always cause smiles in others.

A Provider is loyal to a fault, strongly interested in being of service but often found in a quasi leadership role. The "strong" sibling, for example, or the quarterback – somewhere they can be seen easily and can use their infectious happiness to offer the same to others.

These are the peacemakers in large gatherings and often the hosts, taking great pleasure in seeing a whole room full of people enjoying themselves. They can be easily hurt and are not great fans of spontaneity or unstructured events, but when left to shine they do so with a bright light nobody can ignore.

ISTJ – The Facilitator

Another large group of about the same size as the Defenders, the Facilitator personality type is all about duty and reliability. They are the rocks you can always rely on and the heart of any project.

A Facilitator is incredibly organized, unfailingly logical and inherently sensible. They believe in structure and order and come across as more serious than many of the other personality types.

They will plow through a task without pause, from start to finish, which makes them wonderful team members in pursuit of a long term goal. Their sense of duty will also compel them to do that task to the best of their ability and with patience and diligence at all times.

Facilitators make their decisions based on empirical data and will seek as much information as possible before deciding on an opinion. Their practical nature makes them very goal oriented and impatient with distractions and fanciful activities.

This type of personality is a workhorse, which can sometimes mean they are taken for granted by others. They really are just that reliable – if you want a job done, this is the person to ask. They do, however, need to feel that their work is important and heading towards an overall achievement, and they do need to be able to make sense of that goal and understand how it can be practically applied.

ESTJ – The Executive

If you're looking to establish orderliness, the Executive is you biggest ally. This personality type understands what is right and wrong and believes deeply in tradition, which they use to bring people together.

An Executive is often valued for giving good advice and guiding others towards the right decision. They are often found organizing projects and activities within their community and pushing traditional events and ceremonies that they feel should be cherished.

The Executive believes in law, order and authority and this personality type – which actually represents almost 11 percent of the population – has often been seen in U.S. presidents. These people lead through their own example and are both honest and extremely dedicated.

An Executive does not see the shades of gray and relies on facts and figures to inform their decisions. They follow a moral code that is both unshakeable and derived from the traditions of society – hence why they are so prized as leaders by Western democracies.

You'll hear a person who falls into this category described as a "pillar of the community" or a traditionalist. There is a way of things, they believe, and it ought to be respected. Hard workers with extraordinary integrity, they shine best when bringing others together in pursuit of a goal that will benefit all.

ISFP – The Artist

This personality type couldn't be more of a mirror image to the Executive if it tried. For an Artist, everything is about pushing limits and living life to the full, questioning everything about the status quo and refusing to accept traditions.

An Artist is all about experiences and sensations and seeing the world through their own, unique eyes. On the other hand, they are unlikely to attempt to impose this world view on others. Unlike the Executive, they believe in a "live and let live" philosophy and do not attempt to push others to follow their own ethos.

Devoted to the people they care about and often very considerate, the Artist is spontaneous, unpredictable and not the most reliable of the personality types. They can be tremendous fun as companions if you are able to set aside limits and go with their flow. However, as introverts, they are less visible to the world as a whole than their extravert peers and are often found reflecting on their world in isolation.

Artists in every way, you'll find these people following creative pursuits – sometimes many of them, one after another, as their spontaneous nature refuses to let them settle on one thing. So strong is their drive to experience and enjoy that they can be self centered and blind to the needs of those around them. However, if given the chance to explore that curiosity properly, they can bring incredible works to bear and contribute in meaningful and unique ways to humanity.

ESFP – The Entertainer

If an Entertainer had to be summed up in one word, it would probably be "excitable". They are energetic and enthusiastic, often getting caught up in the moment, and they want to share these things with those around them.

You'll find the Entertainer firmly in the spotlight, putting on a show for their friends and acquaintances and often pursuing careers in the entertainment field, unsurprisingly. They stand out from the crowd with big, bold actions and bold, vibrant clothing – everything about them attracts the eye.

However, the Entertainer can be easily misunderstood. Contrary to appearances, their ability to entertain is not all about getting attention for themselves. They are strongly motivated by a desire to make other people happy and make sure everyone around them is having fun.

They are sensitive to how you are feeling and not much gets past their observant eye. If you have a problem, you can take it to an Entertainer and feel sure that you will be given a strong shoulder and plenty of good advice.

Selflessness is not the Entertainer's downfall, but willingness to knuckle down and tackle the less exciting parts of life very much is. Where you find an Entertainer, you will also find unpaid bills, a repulsion for run-of-the-mill occupations and a lack of focus over time. Pair this person with a more organized personality type, however, and you really do have a recipe for an enjoyable life with all its luxurious trimmings.

ISTP – The Engineer

Nothing pleases an Engineer more than the opportunity to build, design and renovate. This personality type will head straight for the heart of a problem with the goal of finding the best way to begin going about repairs. Not surprisingly, they are usually found in engineering fields.

The Engineer is a quiet soul, usually found exploring how things work and understanding systems because they are highly attracted to structure and enthused by how the world works.

Though Engineers hate wasting time, they do enjoy finding novel approaches and will always listen to your ideas. They will act suddenly to fix or build, making it seem to others as though they are haphazard, but actually they have come to a conclusion quietly and internally about the best way to go about a task.

Engineers love learning, but not from a book. They want to get their hands dirty and pull things apart to look at the insides. Allow them to be as inquisitive as their nature demands and give them a complex problem to solve and they will be truly happy – and perfectly willing to explain what they are doing.

Only five people in every hundred fall into this category, but this personality type is still the one that builds the world around us. Practical and thoughtful, they can have a difficult time understanding emotions and will focus more on your actions to grasp where you are coming from.

ESTP – The Entrepreneur

Life is an adventure for the Entrepreneur. This personality type can be the life of the party and the center of attention and is seldom regarded as shy. They are also the extreme risk takers of the world, seldom looking before they leap and hating to remain idle when they could be out there doing something new and making change.

This is because the Entrepreneur has a logical mind that needs to be stimulated. They enjoy making decisions fast and furiously, based on the facts that are immediately obvious to them. They dislike organized environments, preferring to think outside the box and break the rules for the sake of getting things done.

It's easy to get sucked into the whirlwind of an Entrepreneur – these are people it's easy to like with ideas that sound exciting and fulfilling. They aren't the world's orators, because talking about something just gets in the way of going out and doing it, but they do flourish as the life of any party.

Challenge an Entrepreneur and they will prove themselves up to the task. Ask them to change the status quo and they will do it. Once this personality type has fixated on a goal, there is little they will not do to see it achieved.

The Things that Make Us Unique

As we've spoken about already, figuring out which personality box a person fits into will only tell you a certain amount about who they are. It's certainly a lot more than you knew before you began your analysis, but it's not the whole story.

In many situations, it's perfectly specific enough. If you want your analysis to go further in depth, however, there are certain signals you can look for that will tell you more about the person's unique nature. The first of these involves the beliefs that each of us has about ourselves:

- **Strengths on show:** Each of us is proud of some of the traits we possess. Perhaps the person you are talking to makes amazing cakes and never misses a deadline. As you talk to her, and ask questions to encourage her to open up, you notice that she talks willingly about her cake making and often mentions times when she was pressed to finish something on time but managed it. We love to talk about our perceived strengths, whether or not we consciously mean to do so, because these are the traits we really want other people to know us for. Simply talking to a person and paying attention to the direction he or she leads the conversation in will tell you a great deal about the traits that he or she wants you to notice. It won't just come out in the words a person says, either: watch for the signals they are consciously trying to give. A person dressed in expensive clothes with plenty of jewelry and good shoes, for instance, may want you to think of them as rich. These kinds of "strengths" are important to that person, so they will enjoy your company more and think of you more positively if you encourage them to talk about them and you can win their hearts by respecting their point of view, encouraging them in these areas and listening well.

- Hidden weaknesses: Conversely, each of us feels that we have weaknesses that we would prefer other people do not know about – especially people we respect and like. These are more difficult to spot in a quick conversation but, over time, you'll start to notice them. The weaknesses we perceive in ourselves are not necessarily our actual weaknesses – simply things we do not feel very proud of. For instance, a person might be completely blind to the fact that they are constantly interrupting other people during a conversation, but they may be ashamed of the fact that they are always tardy (even though it's only ever by a couple of minutes and very few of their acquaintances have ever noticed). This, in turn, tells you that punctuality is something that is important to them and that they feel their weakness in that area is likely to cause others to judge them negatively. Perhaps the person you are talking to is ashamed of something about their appearance, a behavior they indulge in that they think people will judge them for or a personality flaw they believe they display. You'll notice that people tend to become defensive or over explain when discussing a perceived weakness. As time goes on, you may also notice as they attempt to hide evidence of this weakness from you and other people. When you are aware of these hidden weaknesses, you can encourage that person to overcome them or accept them, ingratiating yourself immensely to them in the process.

- **Driving Forces:** What we believe to be our strengths and weaknesses have a habit of driving our behavior. Our ambitions, goals and general attitude to life is often molded from our attempts to overcome what we think of as our weaknesses while playing to our strengths. Once you have figured out what a person thinks of as their strengths, you'll be able to understand better what they want to do and be in life. For instance, someone who thinks their primary trait is intelligence may aspire to be a college lecturer and may feel compelled to drive the conversation about intellectual topics during a gathering. You can use this knowledge to support a person in their endeavors and compliment them on their successes. On the other side of the coin, you can see as their perceived weaknesses influence their choices in the opposite direction, driving them away from certain behaviors instead of towards them. If a person feels ashamed of their weight, for example, he or she may avoid the spotlight, find places to stand or sit where they will be less easily seen and avoid any situation where a weight limit is likely or a chair is "too small". Help that person understand that you see them as beautiful and interesting and that their weight has nothing to do with your perception of them and you'll win a friend for life.

Firstborn, Second Born, Baby of the Family: The Role of Birth Order

The role that we take in our nuclear family as we are growing up has a distinct impact on who we become as an adult. Whether a person is the baby of the family or the firstborn can profoundly influence how their personality develops.

For this reason, as part of your analysis, asking if a person has any brothers or sisters can be wonderfully revealing. You can combine the knowledge of how that person fit into their family with your analysis of their personality type to draw tentative conclusions about them.

First Child

The first child in a family is usually the one on whom all the parental expectations are placed – it's no cliché that mom and dad have usually relaxed by the time baby number two comes along. A first child will therefore usually be a perfectionist and ambitious and will also be relatively reliable. They tend to be motivated and focused on achievement and very determined to see things through. Many have high self-confidence, too.

Middle Child

This title applies to any sibling who wasn't born first or last, regardless of whether there are three siblings in the family. The middle child is often the polar opposite of the first child as less attention was given to them now that mom and dad have settled into childrearing. They can be insecure, attention seekers, independent, rebellious and sometimes quite secretive.

Last Child

The baby of the family is often given the most love of all – not because their parents love them better, but because they also have elder siblings to adore them. They tend to be less able to take responsibility, more carefree and happy go lucky and sometimes a little spoiled. This makes them both fun and warm to spend time with and self centered, expecting more attention and love than others.

Only Child

An only child has a similar personality to the firstborn child as they, too, will have received undivided attention from their parents. They may also be more private than others, as they did not have to share, and less confident in forming relationships and taking part in social gatherings than those who grew up with a constant social whirlwind taking place in their very own home.

A Person's Beliefs

The final piece of the puzzle when it comes to figuring out the basic building blocks of the person you are analyzing is their belief system. These are the beliefs that a person holds thanks to their personality and the experiences they have had along the way. It's what we each believe is possible, fair and correct – and also what we believe is not.

Our core beliefs are the ones that are the most difficult to change because we hold them right in the center of our hearts. You can tell what a person believes to be the right way to act, think and be by the kinds of conversation topics they show interest in.

You can also look out for themes in their speech; for example, if someone believes in their core that contributing to the community is something every person will do, they will speak often and enthusiastically about instances where they or someone else did exactly that.

Core beliefs tell you a lot about how that person perceives the world and what makes them happy and content. Your subject's core beliefs tell you plenty about how they believe they should act and think, which in turn helps you predict their thoughts and actions. Listen for those repeating themes and for signs that their belief systems have impacted their conclusions on events around them. For example, someone who believes that honesty is vital is going to be much more offended by a lying politician.

We also each possess what are known as "limiting beliefs" – the thoughts that hold us back. For example, someone might tell you that they would desperately love to be a teacher but that they're not intelligent enough to do a good job; or that they thought about being a journalist while growing up but they didn't think they'd be able to write well enough. Statements such as this tell you what a person believes he or she is not – and what fears might be holding them back from their true potential.

Finally, we have more general beliefs, such as our belief in cultural norms, religion, political affiliation and economic status. A person who grew up rich will believe different things to someone who grew up poor, while someone who practices the Jewish faith will hold different beliefs than someone who grew up as a Muslim. These general beliefs can be gleaned through simple questions about the person's background.

One last thing to watch out for during your analysis: a reaction that a person gives to something you say or do that they simply cannot help. Each of us has a set of triggers that link to things that make us happy, sad, stressed, frightened and so on.

These will manifest as unconscious reactions that seem to be either too strong to fit the current situation (such as showing extreme fear when a door slams, which could relate to a frightening experience in the person's past) or don't fit with it at all (such as seeming angry when you mention cats). Whether or not you feel comfortable enough with the person in that moment to mention the anomalous behavior or you'd prefer to store it for later exploration is up to you and the context of your conversation, but be sure to take mental note of these unconscious triggers when you see them.

Cold Readings

The building blocks can tell us who a person was born to be, but life experiences are a significant part of what makes each of us unique. Two people may be born equally generous, but one of those people may be held in great esteem for it while the other finds themselves swindled out of their life savings by a ruthless criminal. As you can imagine, the two of them will have very different opinions about the role of generosity in their lives – and whether it's a strength or a weakness.

During your analysis, as we mentioned at the end of the last chapter, it's important to gather information about the person's background. Facts can be as important as feelings when it comes to figuring a person out. Their socioeconomic status, religion, cultural background, politics and more can tell you about their experiences. These experiences will help to shape who a person is and, because the development of personality is cyclical, will also help you understand how the conclusions the person drew then helped to further shape their character.

At this point in your analysis, you have a pretty good idea of the basic personality type you are dealing with – but how has life influenced that personality along the way? To find out more – and also to help you figure out those strengths, weaknesses and motivations that set this person apart – you can use what's known as "cold readings" – the same technique that so-called psychics often use to make it seem like they know more about a person than they really do.

Human beings like to identify with things personally – we seek ways to apply information directly to ourselves. That's why so many people are taken in by horoscopes, even though a statement such as, "love will play a major role in your life today" could mean almost anything.

You can use these kinds of statements to draw out information from your subject. Using everything you have learned about the person so far, make general statements or ask general questions that will encourage them to open up further. Some examples might be:

- "It sounds as though you've had an intense few years"

- "I get the feeling that XXX is very important to you"
- "You tend to be critical of yourself, don't you?"
- "It seems like you've had some doubts about the decisions you've made recently"
- "You keep the real you hidden from other people"
- "You seem to think of yourself as an independent thinker"

These are some of the statements that psychologists teach as part of the "Barnum Effect" – the idea that we can be taken in by such blanket statements because we want to apply them to ourselves on a personal level. It's named after a showman – the one who coined the term, "there's a sucker born every minute".

Obviously, the real Barnum felt that techniques like cold reading were a great way to con the people around him. However, it's just as useful when you genuinely want to get the measure of a person and need them to open up to you.

As the conversation progresses, you will learn more information about the person and can use that information to formulate your next statement or question. The key is to limit your own contribution to the conversation to just these Barnum statements. Don't worry – your subject won't think of you as closed off or uncommunicative. The more you "get them right", the more they will think of you as perceptive and a potential ally.

Reading Body Language

What we say and what we mean can sometimes be two very different things, and that's where body language comes in. Because body language makes up the vast majority of communication, no book on analyzing people would be complete without a guide to reading it more accurately.

Only 7% of what we say comes through in our actual words – the remaining 93% is to be found in our tone, volume, posture, movements, facial expressions and more. You'll find hundreds of guides to body language on the book shelves, but what we're interested in when it comes to analyzing people is very specific.

We want to understand a person's body language baseline: how they speak and stand when they are completely relaxed. When we know this, we can spot the signs of a change in that relaxed state. This can be incredibly helpful during an analysis because it means we can read between the lines – which is especially useful when we are figuring out motivations and weaknesses that the person may not ever describe in words.

Body language is so important to an analysis that it's safe to say you will never take an accurate read without it. However, we've left it until this stage of the book for a very important reason: before you can use it to make judgments, you need the person to be comfortable with you.

Only when a person is fully relaxed in your company, no longer suspicious of you and your motivation and able to trust you as a confidant will you begin to see how they hold themselves and communicate in that relaxed state. You need to know this because it will be your baseline. This is the person's "normal" in the context in which you are speaking to them and any change from it will be an anomaly that gives you an idea of what they are really thinking.

For example, let's say that the person you are analyzing tells you they absolutely love their job and wouldn't change it for the world. Because you got them to say this through a Barnum statement, you are fairly confident it's true. However, you notice that their body language changes as they say it, becoming more closed and tense. Now your interpretation changes – you know that this statement is either something they want you to believe or that they don't feel safe telling you the truth.

This is also where context comes in. Let's say you're at an informal party with mutual friends and nobody is around who works with this person. That's a very different situation to hearing someone claim they adore their job while at a work function where their boss might overhear. Keep context in the back of your mind when analyzing body language – it might give you even more information than you were hoping for. It's also important to realize that the baseline you're seeing in this context may change slightly if you talk again in another context, so be prepared to adjust your concept of their baseline the next time you see them.

So, why are we looking for anomalies? Because body language is an unconscious signal that can reveal the truth behind a person's words. For instance, perhaps you mention how everyone turns into a bit of a wild child in their university years and the person's body language instantly becomes uncomfortable and less confident. That tells you something happened during this person's years as a student that may bear further investigation. Or, perhaps the person claims that they go to church every Sunday and wouldn't miss it for the world, but their body language changes as they say this. This can tell you that the person may be lying, perhaps to impress you or because they believe it's what you want to hear or perhaps to hide a perceived weakness.

In general, you're looking for signs of tension and discomfort to spot that someone is either not telling the truth or has become uncomfortable with the conversation. If a person's body language becomes more expansive and open, on the other hand, you can assume enthusiasm for the topic.

Some of these signs include:

- Crossed arms: If the person crosses their arms in front of them, they are "defending" themselves and either disagree with you or is feeling the need to defend themselves.

- Nose touching: A strange one, to be sure, but a person who touches their nose is often lying to you or rejecting your opinion.

- Nodding: This one is pleasingly obvious. If a person nods along with you as you speak, then they agree with you.

- Fiddling: If the person begins picking at themselves, biting their nails or similar, they are expressing a nervous habit that suggests they are feeling stressed or confused.

- Eye contact: When we are comfortable and open, we make eye contact with the person we are talking to. If we lose that comfort level for some reason, we find it more difficult to maintain the eye contact.

- Looking down: A person who lowers their gaze to the floor is either lying to you or for some reason feeling shy.

- Looking to the side: If the person looks to the side when breaking eye contact rather than looking down, then they have likely lost interest in the conversation – time to move it on to new topics.

- Pointing: We point when we are trying to take charge, often if we want to express authority over another person. This tends to happen if we are feeling angry or threatened in some way.

- Smile: We all know the meanings of a smile, when they are genuine. If you do not observe the smile "reaching their eyes" and causing wrinkles to appear in the muscles around the eyes as well as the mouth, then the smile is not genuine and the person may be uncomfortable or insincere.

- Clenched hands: If the person tightens their hands into a fist, they are annoyed or angry. This can also indicate frustration if the person is trying hard to get a point across but doesn't feel it is being heard.

- Pursed lips: If a person purses or clenches their lips together, then they are uncomfortable with what they are saying. Often they are making a confession they would prefer not to have to make and will avoid telling the whole truth if they can.

- Rubbing hands: When someone rubs their hands together unconsciously, they are usually excited about something.

- Tone of voice: Our tone changes unconsciously, so if you notice the person's voice lowering then they are sad or bored, while if it rises then we are excited or enthused.

- Voice speed: When a person's voice speeds up, they are often nervous about something and want to reach the end of their sentence to convince you of what they are trying to say.

- Body "up" or "down": When we are excited and interested in the conversation, we raise various body parts including arms and chins and heads – sometimes even legs. When a person feels uncomfortable, bored or chastised, they will droop downwards instead.

- Moving feet: A sure sign of discomfort is a waving or jiggling foot. This is a response to feeling a "fight or flight" reaction – our feet want us to move and react, but socially we cannot do this, so our feet unconsciously move anyway, partly to expel the excess energy caused by adrenaline.

- Pointing: Pay attention to whether a person is leaning towards you and whether their feet and legs are directed your way. If they are, that person is absorbed in the conversation and interested in you. If their feet or torso turn away, they have lost interest or want to "escape".

- Body position: If the person has relaxed into their chair and crossed their legs, getting comfortable, or has crossed their legs to get settled while standing, then they are planning to stick around for a while and are comfortable in the conversation. If they show signs of poising themselves to leave, such as moving to the edge of the seat or leaning away in the direction they plan to move, then they are no longer comfortable or interested and want to leave.

As you can see, there are plenty of signals to keep an eye out for, most of which are easy to notice when you've familiarized yourself with the baseline. You can use these signals to spot lies, tell when someone is truly enjoying the topic at hand, uncomfortable with the direction of the conversation and much more, allowing you to decipher their words on a much deeper level.

The most important thing to take away from this chapter is the idea of finding that baseline. Most body language guides will swear blind that X body movement means Y, but that's simply not the truth – everyone, as we know, is different. What you are looking for are anomalies, which will give you a broad indication of a person's state of mind that will allow you to analyze their reactions in context.

Detecting Specific Personality Traits Through Body Language

There is some debate in psychological circles as to whether you can use body language analysis to predict what personality type a person has according to the Myers Briggs model. While our interactions with the world are very much dictated by who we are and how we think, it's important to bear in mind that we are also strongly influenced by our surroundings, the culture we are part of and other social cues.

So while you may be tempted to turn to body language as the major part of your analysis, it's probably not going to give you as accurate a read as you were hoping. In fact, it's highly likely that you will get the wrong impression entirely, unless you factor in these aspects.

On the other hand, it would be wrong to dismiss body language entirely, because there really will be signals waiting to be noticed. Body language is therefore best used to confirm what you think you have already deduced – a confirmation tool, in other words.

In general, you will find that:

- Extraverts are seldom quiet in a social setting and will often dominate the conversation. Pay attention to how your subject interacts not just with you, but also in larger group conversations and when greeting new people as they enter your conversation circle. An extravert tends to be the one who wants to interact with everyone and will encourage people to join their conversation. They will locate themselves towards the center of the room or circle between groups of people and will be expansive in their gestures. This may manifest as a louder voice than those around them – one that tends to carry across the room – or arm gestures and an animated face. They will also show much less reservation when it comes to making eye contact. Watch others' body language too: some of the personality types with extravert included are magnetic and command attention, so you'll notice that others will turn their bodies and therefore attention in the extravert's direction.

- Introverts are less comfortable in a social setting and will not be as adept at small talk and attracting the attention of others – even if they try. Some introverts can very much be described as a "people person" but will often grow quieter and more reserved the bigger their audience. On the other hand, take care to include other information in analyzing an introvert as there are certain personality types in which the introversion takes a back seat to a desire to make others happy and comfortable. In these cases, the introvert will still likely show some of the signals of feeling overwhelmed by large social situations, such as sticking to the edges of the room wherever possible and preferring conversations with a small number of people rather than a large group. They may also show defensive body language gestures, such as folding their arms in front of themselves, making eye contact less often and keeping their gestures small to deflect attention.

- Sensing people can sometimes be spotted through their eyes. Because they make most of their decisions based on sensory input, they are wired to always be seeking it. If your subject appears to be looking around them at the room and the people in it, noticing everything, then they are likely to have sensing as a trait. They will also show body language signals of interest, such as opening up their body language by dropping crossed arms and leaning towards you, when you turn the conversation towards topics that interest them, such as current events and pop culture. The opposite will be true if you talk about subjects such as philosophy, which bore them – after leaving a suitable pause for politeness, they may appear to withdraw into themselves, allowing their attention to wander back to what is happening around them in the room or allowing their eyes to glaze over.

- Intuitive people don't usually come across as quite so observant of what's going on around them. Their eyes will likely remain fixed within a small area of the room and will dart around less. They can sometimes come across as slightly spaced out in a social situation. The conversation test works in reverse here: if you are speaking to an intuitive, they will become engaged, their eyes will light up and their body language will open up if you tackle subjects such as philosophy and politics, as these will capture their attention. (Of course, in both cases, be wary of making assumptions until you've hit on a conversation topic that genuinely interests them – an intuitive is not necessarily going to be fascinated by the state of the European Union and a sensing person is not necessarily interested in the latest Marvel movie, so try a few topics if the first doesn't give you a good read.)

- A feeling person is likely to be the one who is smiling and laughing a lot and generally showing their emotion on their face. To tell a feeling person, watch for facial expressions in response to the story they are either telling or being told, as they will generally react by displaying the appropriate emotion (shock, sadness, amusement etc.). Feeling people often have loud laughs and big smiles and their state of mind can easily be seen on their face.

- Thinking people are much less likely to allow their emotions to be read on their faces. They come across as calmer, with their movements and facial expressions more controlled and less likely to be triggered by a reaction to what someone else is saying. This can sometimes make them seem "colder" than their feeling cousins.

- To spot a judging person, take a look at their appearance. Clothing, hair, jewelry, accessories, shoes, makeup – all of these things can be body language signals of their own. A judging person pays more attention to this physical manifestation of themselves and will appear to be more neat and tidy and more "put together". Their outfit will fit well, be clean and tidy and will be appropriate for the occasion.

- Perceivers are the opposite of judging people in their appearance. They can often be spotted through their slightly unkempt nature – tops falling off shoulders, slightly frayed handbags, creases on their shirts, messy hair and other small flaws in their outfit and appearance that indicate they didn't pay quite as much attention to it as they could have.

As you can see, there are signals for every personality factor – it's up to you to make sure you are reading them correctly and incorporating them into your analysis as a supporting factor that helps you be certain you know who you are dealing with.

Detecting Lies

Body language has a second, very important function for an analyst. Up until now, we've been mostly assuming that everything our subject tells us is the truth. Now that we've incorporated body language into our analysis, we can use it to detect those statements that are not entirely accurate.

Human beings are almost always trying to make a good impression, whatever that may take. It's important to our own self esteem and our vision of ourselves that the person we are talking to both likes us and has a positive view of us.

Particularly when we are talking about our perceived weaknesses, a true statement brings the danger of threatening that positive impression. If, for example, your subject thinks of themselves as lazy and does not want you to know about that perceived weakness, they may tell you that they visit the gym every day, spend at least an hour each day on personal goals such as diary writing or are passionate about doing their work to the best of their ability.

Just because these statements are lies doesn't mean that person is a liar – and it doesn't make these statements less valuable to your analysis. You are interested in a person's perceived weaknesses just as much as their perceived strengths, after all.

For this reason, becoming a human lie detector is an incredibly useful skill for an analyst. Some of the signals you'll want to watch for (once again bearing in mind that all-important baseline) are:

- Looking up and to the right: When a person does this, it's an unconscious signal of a lie because their face is reflecting which part of the brain they are activating. The person is making up a response, rather than recollecting information. Be aware that a left handed person often looks up and to the left instead.

- Loss of eye contact or blinking: When a person lies, they will try to "hide" from you by blinking for extended periods or looking away, almost as though they believe that the truth is visible in their eyes and you won't "see" it if you can't see into them. It's a little like a toddler thinking you can't see them if they cover their eyes and can't see you.

- Dilated pupils: This often happens completely unconsciously while a lie is being told.

- Nervous gestures: Clearing the throat, fiddling with clothes and other signs of nervousness indicate that the person is worried they will be caught in the lie.

- Head moving backwards: Telling a lie invokes nervousness and fear, which the brain naturally reacts to by attempting to remove the person from the source of that nervousness and fear. This often manifests in a moving of the head backwards and away from you, to "distance" the person.

- Swallowing: Another side effect of fear and nervousness is a dry throat, which can sometimes cause the person to repeatedly swallow.

Danger Signals

Analyzing people is an effective tool when it comes to making friends, influencing people and making better impression on new acquaintances, but it has another important use that may one day mean the difference between life and death. A successful analysis can also help you spot the signs of danger before harm ever comes to you or the people around you.

For a psychopath, criminal or killer, or even a person who is unable to control their aggression and anger, the fact that we usually take our first impressions for granted is the very basis of their success. These people rely on the fact that we make superficial judgments and then fail to dig any deeper – that's precisely how they fool us.

A person might be a serial killer behind closed doors but, as long as they take out the trash on time and always have a smile for their neighbor's kids, most people will assume they are a pleasant and normal human being. These people make use of the fact that most of us are not analysts to hide who they really are.

But you are an analyst – you are now equipped with the skills to look past the superficial. That means you have a better chance than most to see the warning signs that a person is gearing up to do something harmful and remove yourself from a potentially dangerous situation.

It's not a foolproof science so please do be aware that you should always trust your gut instinct and excuse yourself from a person's company, even if you're not sure the signs are really there. It's also important to never assume you've read a person correctly and then fail to take the measures you normally would to protect yourself from harm. Consider this no more than an additional weapon in your self-protection kit.

There are a number of common red flags to be aware of. One of these, in the right context, might mean nothing at all. Two is a warning sign – three or four is a sure sign you should remove yourself from a situation as quickly as you can.

- Dilated pupils: When this happens in a situation of even minor conflict, take note. This person's body has released adrenaline and there is a danger that they will soon move past polite disagreement into aggression and possibly violent acts.

- Arousal signs: Another involuntary signal that a person is about to engage in some kind of aggressive or violent act is the color of their skin. The body's reaction is to get the blood pumping and this will lead to flushed skin and pulsing veins. You may also note that the person perspires, their eyes widen so that you can see more of the whites and their breathing quickens.

- Hand movements: Clenched fists, as we mentioned earlier, is a sign of anger. If the person's hands are reaching into a pocket or bag, they may be seeking a weapon. Make sure you are always aware of what the hands are doing even while watching a person's face. Never forget that the hands are the tools with which we interact with the world – and also the weapons.

- Rigidity: A person who is angry or preparing to do violence will often become very rigid, particularly in the shoulder region. This may be coupled with a widening of the legs as the person takes a fighting stance.

These warning signals, of course, will only protect you from a violent person at the moment they decide to turn on you. As you get to know a person who is hiding a secret predilection for violence or abuse, you may also notice subtle signals that all is not exactly as you thought.

For example, dangerous people tend to be pushy and want to become more involved in your life than you feel comfortable with – and will often react strongly if you do not allow this. They seek quick attachments with no real basis.

They may also ask you questions that seem too nosy for the level of your relationship and they may lie often about things that seem inconsequential, such as whether they enjoy cheese. They have short tempers, but are quick to become charming once again, and lack the ability to empathize with your feelings and experiences.

No two dangerous people are the same, any more than two normal people are the same, but your analysis skills may help you to weed out the less desirable friends and acquaintances before they sink their hooks into you. Again: listen to your gut and never ignore a strange piece of behavior, even if you can't explain it or it seems unbelievable that it might mean the person you're speaking to is not as pleasant as they seem.

A Final Word: Listening to Really Hear

With the techniques we have covered in this book, you possess the knowledge to learn about another person within a single conversation – and to truly get to know them as time goes by.

You may have noticed that a single skill ties the entire process together. While it's important to hone your observational skills and take note of body language and signals, analysis relies almost entirely on the ability to listen.

This isn't a skill that most of us naturally possess. Most of us listen simply to await our turn to speak, rather than to really hear what the other person is telling us. An analyst can't afford to begin a conversation with the goal of speaking – you must practice your listening skills until you are perfectly content to simply listen to another person, hear what they are telling you and the subtext hiding behind it and press them to continue speaking once they are done.

Why are most people so bad at analyzing others? Because, for the most part, we are only hearing around 25 percent of what is said to us. Most of us are missing out on an incredibly 75 percent of the information on offer – and that's not going to be good enough if you truly want to understand another human being.

There's a reason that good listeners are valued so highly in human society. It's such a rare skill to simply listen – and to really hear – that we take note when we find someone able and willing to do it. Rest assured that becoming a good listener will do nothing to harm other people's opinion of you. On the contrary, it will endear you to almost everyone you meet along the way.

A good listener to not just hear the words being said, but to actively pay attention to them and the nonverbal cues that come alongside. A good listener does not drift off into considering their response, because you are not interested in responding with anything more than a prompt for your subject to continue.

A good listener does not get distracted by the sights and sounds around them any more than you allow yourself to be distracted by the funny story you want to tell when your subject finishes their sentence. A good listener does not allow their thoughts to wander away from the conversation because it's not stimulating you – in fact, a good analyst is seldom bored by what they are hearing because new information about the subject is their very bread and butter.

Don't worry if listening doesn't come naturally to you – for almost everyone, it's a skill that needs honing. As you begin to put your knowledge of analysis into practice in your social life, love life and work situation, you can continue your practice of listening at the same time.

We think of human beings as mysterious creatures, but that's mostly because there is such an incredibly variety of traits and characteristics within a single personality and an almost infinite number of combinations. As a species, we are so wonderfully diverse that each one of us is utterly unique.

But that doesn't mean we can't develop an understanding of one another on a deep level. An analyst knows that their work is never really done, that there's always something new to discover about a person and add into their ongoing analysis. An analyst also knows that there are few things so fulfilling as understanding another person and what drives them and using that knowledge to both forge a strong connection and help their new friend, lover, colleague or acquaintance succeed in whatever they choose to pursue.